Society Massachusetts Historical

Commemoration of the four hundredth anniversary of the

birth of Martin Luther

.

Society Massachusetts Historical

Commemoration of the four hundredth anniversary of the birth of Martin Luther

ISBN/EAN: 9783337126834

Printed in Europe, USA, Canada, Australia, Japan

Cover: Foto ©Lupo / pixelio.de

More available books at **www.hansebooks.com**

Massachusetts Historical Society.

·

COMMEMORATION

OF THE

FOUR HUNDREDTH ANNIVERSARY

OF

BIRTH OF MARTIN LUTHER,

November 10, 1883.

COMMEMORATION

OF THE

FOUR HUNDREDTH ANNIVERSARY

OF

THE BIRTH OF MARTIN LUTHER,

BY THE

𝔐𝔞𝔰𝔰𝔞𝔠𝔥𝔲𝔰𝔢𝔱𝔱𝔰 𝔥𝔦𝔰𝔱𝔬𝔯𝔦𝔠𝔞𝔩 𝔖𝔬𝔠𝔦𝔢𝔱𝔶,

NOVEMBER 10, 1883.

BOSTON:
PUBLISHED BY THE SOCIETY.
M.DCCC.LXXXIII.

CONTENTS.

———◆———

COMMEMORATION

OF

THE BIRTH OF MARTIN LUTHER.

AT a meeting of the MASSACHUSETTS HISTORICAL SOCIETY held on Thursday, June 14, 1883, Dr. GEORGE E. ELLIS said : —

The tenth day of November next will complete four centuries since the birth of Martin Luther. The signal influence of his life and career, among the most effective forces working through Christendom in that extended period of time, will find fitting recognition and observance in various parts of Europe. His own fatherland, rightfully taking the lead in grateful and elaborate offices of commemoration, will stir sympathetic observances among all the most advanced peoples on continent or island. On this northern half of the then New World — which, at the era of the birth of the great reformer, was veiled in darkness soon to be irradiated—there are millions of our race who will not be content with any merely responsive echo of foreign notes. It is eminently fitting that this Society, the oldest in the country in its special objects, should take not only a leading, but a prompting part, in promoting and securing such a recognition of that birthday as is in perfect harmony with our aims, — secular indeed, but not oblivious of higher interests. It offers us the broadest and most comprehensive themes and aspects, political, intellectual, philosophical, ecclesiastical, and popular.

Happily we have with us one who was for many years our associate in this Society, and a Professor in the University, — a German scholar, profoundly versed in the literature, the philosophy, the history, science, art, and broadest culture of the birth-land of Luther; and who is gifted with especial talents, with breadth of thought, and compass of view, for a brilliant rehearsal of his career, and of his place in the world's history and in the higher development of humanity.   I would therefore propose to the Society the following motion : —

That we invite Dr. Frederic H. Hedge to prepare an address for delivery in some public hall in this city, on the 10th of November next, commemorative of the life, the career, and the influence of Martin Luther.

That the officers of this Society be a committee to make all the proper arrangements for the occasion.

The Resolution was adopted.

At a stated meeting held on October 11th, the President announced that the Council had decided that the exercises in commemoration of the four hundredth anniversary of the birth of Luther should be held in Arlington Street Church, on Saturday, November 10, and that Dr. F. H. Hedge would deliver the oration, and Dr. Phillips Brooks would be invited to offer prayer.

The Recording Secretary, and Messrs. Charles C. Smith and Henry W. Haynes were appointed a committee of arrangements.

At a monthly meeting of the Society on November 8th, the Rev. EDWARD J. YOUNG, in behalf of the committee of arrangements, made the following remarks : —

REMARKS

BY THE REV. EDWARD J. YOUNG.

I WISH that we might have been able to procure for the approaching commemoration copies of three portraits of Luther, which represent him at the three great epochs of his life. One of these gives a likeness of him as a monk, wearing a cowl, and with shaven head. Another portrays him as Squire George, with black beard and florid face, disguised in the suit of a knight, — a complete contrast to the other. A third painting is that with which we are all familiar, which represents him as the grave and dignified reformer. So different are these three portraitures, that they hardly seem to delineate the same person.

I should be glad, also, if we could have obtained a picture of the Augustinian cloister at Erfurt, before it was destroyed by fire in 1872, where Friar Martin said his first mass and underwent his severe monastic discipline, and gained that experience and knowledge which enabled him to take up his pen against the Papal Church. As a companion-piece to this, I should like to have had a representation of the old castle of the Wartburg, as it stands in the most romantic part of the Thuringian forest, whither Luther was conveyed for safety, after the Diet at Worms, by order of the Elector of Saxony, and where he passed ten months in that asylum which he called his "Patmos." No scenes which I have ever visited have awakened more thrilling emotions than the cell in which he did penance as a priest, and the chamber in which he translated the New Testament, while visited by the Evil One.

Since it has been impossible to find in this country these views, however, it may be interesting for the members of

the Society to see a copy of Luther's famous tract, which I
brought many years ago from Germany, and which is entitled
" Against the Papacy at Rome, founded by the Devil.   Wittenberg, 1545." It is printed in Old German, and in black
letter ; and on the titlepage is an extraordinary picture of the
Pope going down into the jaws of hell, while demons on all
sides are punching and jeering at him.   Nothing better at-
tests the fearless, defiant spirit of the author, than that he
dared to put such a frontispiece to his treatise, which in the
plainest terms attacks and confutes the pretensions of the
Papacy.   I will read one or two passages from this work, as I
am not aware that it has ever been translated.   It begins by
speaking of the Holy Father as the " Most Hellish Father,"
and he is uniformly addressed in it as " Your Hellishness,"
instead of " Your Holiness."   After arraigning him through
several pages for denying the right of the Emperor to call a
National Council, and for assuming that he alone has authority to regulate all matters relating to faith and practice,
Luther proceeds : —

" Does any one now think that I am indulging my own pleasure in
employing these sarcastic, choleric, caustic words against the Pope ?
Good Heavens ! I am altogether too feeble to ridicule the Pope.   He
has ridiculed the world for more than six hundred years, and laughed
in his sleeve at its ruin of body and soul, welfare and honor.   And he
still does not cease and cannot cease, for, as St. Peter calls him, he is
' an unceasing, restless, incorrigible sinner ' ('Ακαταπαύστον άμαρτίας,
incessabilem, inquietum, incorrigibiliter peccatorem.   2 Peter ii. 14).
No one could believe what an abomination the Papacy is.   A Christian
must have no small capacity, to be able to comprehend it.   God himself must ridicule it in the fire of hell ; and our Lord Christ, as St.
Paul says (2 Thessalonians ii. 8), must slay it with the breath of his
mouth, and destroy it by his glorious coming.   I ridicule it with my
weak sarcasm simply for this reason, that those who are now living
and who shall come after us may know what I think of the Pope, the
accursed Anti-Christ ; and if any one will be a Christian, let him be
warned from such an abomination."

In the closing paragraph of the book he denounces bitterly
the head of the Church, and thus concludes : —

" But I must stop here. God willing, I will do better in another
little book. Should I die,* however, God grant that another may
make one a thousand fold more severe. For the
devilish Papacy is the greatest curse
on earth, and the worst which
all the devils with all their
power could contrive.
God help us.
Amen."

These words may seem to us violent and excessive ; but
we must bear in mind the monstrous abuses which had been
sanctioned by the Vatican ; the edict of excommunication
which it had issued against Luther ; † and that he was, as he
declared, " rough, boisterous, stormy, and altogether warlike,
born to fight innumerable devils and monsters, to remove
stumps and stones, to cut down thistles and thorns, and to
clear the wild woods."

His private correspondence · with his family and friends,
however, reveals another side of his character. His tender
epistles to his wife, which were the spontaneous utterance of
his heart, in the midst of his fierce conflicts, evince his gentle
and affectionate disposition. His letter to his dear boy, begin-
ning with " Mercy and peace in Christ, my darling son," and
describing a delightful garden in which were a great many
children who had beautiful horses with golden bridles and
silver saddles, was written in 1530, during the proceedings of
the Diet at Augsburg, where the Confession of Faith, prepared
by Melanchthon and approved by Luther, was submitted by
the Protestant princes. A similar tender and loving spirit
pervades the charming Christmas carol which he composed for
his little Hans, and which is sung on every Christmas morning from the dome of the Kreuzkirche in Dresden, as well as
in many Sunday-schools on both sides of the Atlantic.

---

* Luther died in the following year, Feb. 18, 1546.
† " Bulla Leonis X. contra errores Mart. Lutheri, 17 Kalen. Julii, MDXX.
" Adversus execrabilem Antichristi Bullam, Martinus Lutherus, I. Decem-
bris, Anno MDXX."

Among the eminent services rendered by Luther, it must
not be forgotten that he translated the entire Bible alone,
and into such pure and idiomatic speech that it has become
a classic.   He wrote also several commentaries on the
Scriptures, and his complete works in German and Latin
comprise in one edition twenty-four quarto volumes, and in
another more than a hundred octavo volumes.

In one of the churches in the university town of Halle, there
is a medallion head of the Reformer, inscribed "Sanctus Doctor
M. Lutherus, Propheta Germaniæ."   But he was not merely a
prophet; he was a poet, scholar, theologian, preacher, states-
man, as well as a man of affairs, and he belongs not simply
to his own fatherland, but to all Protestant Christendom.

There are four great personages, connected with the past,
whose names still meet and impress the traveller everywhere
throughout Northern Germany.   They are Napoleon, Frederick the Great, Gustavus Adolphus, and Martin Luther.   It
is a testimony to the power and greatness of the last-named,
that, distinguished as are the other three, his fame and worth
do not shrink in comparison with theirs.   Which one of
them will have such universal and grateful recognition on
the four hundredth anniversary of his birthday?   The humble miner's son, who was born on *St. Martin's* eve, and who
became the leader of one of the most important movements
of human history, will be forever remembered as having contributed more than any other individual to the civil and
religious liberty of modern times.

Dr. J. F. CLARKE quoted Dr. Gottheil, rabbi of the Temple Emanuel in New York, as saying that, though not a
thorough Hebrew scholar, Luther had an instinctive divining
power for interpreting the Old Testament.

Judge CHAMBERLAIN said that in the Boston Public
Library there was a volume of Luther with his autograph
in it.

The Society adjourned to meet at 3 o'clock on Saturday,
the 10th instant, in Arlington Street Church.

At the appointed hour a large congregation assembled, and filled the church. The meeting was opened with prayer by the Rev. Phillips Brooks, D.D. The Rev. Louis B. Schwarz, pastor of the German Reformed Church in Boston, then read, in German, Luther's hymn.*

Ein' feste Burg ist unser Gott,
Ein' gute Wehr und Waffen.
Er hilft uns frei aus aller Noth,
Die uns jetzt hat betroffen.
Der alt' böse Feind   Mit Ernst er's jetzt meint;
Groß' Macht und viel List,   Sein grausam' Rüstung ist,
Auf Erd'n ist nicht sein's Gleichen.

Mit unsrer Macht ist nichts gethan,
Wir sind gar bald verloren:
Es streit't für uns der rechte Mann,
Den Gott hat selbst erkoren.
Fragst du, wer Der ist?   Er heißt Jesus Christ,
Der Herr Zebaoth,   Und ist kein andrer Gott;
Das Feld muß Er behalten.

Und wenn die Welt voll Teufel wär
Und wollt uns gar verschlingen,
So fürchten wir uns nicht so sehr,
Es soll uns doch gelingen.
Der Fürst dieser Welt,   Wie sau'r er sich stellt,
Thut Er uns doch nichts;   Das macht, er ist gericht't,
Ein Wörtlein kann ihn fällen.

Das Wort sie sollen lassen stan,†
Und kein'n Dank darzu haben.
Er ist bei uns wohl auf dem Plan‡
Mit seinem Geist und Gaben.
Nehmen sie den Leib,   Gut, Ehr, Kind und Weib;
Laß fahren dahin,   Sie haben's kein'n Gewinn:
Das Reich muß uns doch bleiben!

---

* This hymn is here printed in the form in which it appears in the hymn-book authorized by the Synod of the German Reformed Church in this country, edited by Dr. Philip Schaff.

† stehen.   ‡ Kampfplatz.

An English translation of this hymn by the Rev. Dr. F. H.
Hedge was then sung by the choir, reinforced by the Orpheus
Musical Society, to the original music.

A MIGHTY fortress is our God,
    A bulwark never failing;
Our helper he amid the flood
    Of mortal ills prevailing.
For still our ancient foe
Doth seek to work us woe;
His craft and power are great;
And, armed with cruel hate,
    On earth is not his equal.

Did we in our own strength confide,
    Our striving would be losing;
Were not the right man on our side, —
    The man of God's own choosing.
Dost ask who that may be?
Christ Jesus: it is he;
Lord Sabaoth his name,
From age to age the same,
    And He must win the battle.

And though this world, with devils filled,
    Should threaten to undo us,
We will not fear; for God hath willed
    His truth to triumph through us.
The Prince of Darkness grim, —
We tremble not for him:
His rage we can endure,
For, lo! his doom is sure:
    One little word shall fell him.

That word above all earthly powers —
    No thanks to them — abideth;
The spirit and the gifts are ours,
    Through Him who with us sideth.
Let goods and kindred go,
This mortal life also:
The body they may kill,
God's truth abideth still;
    His kingdom is forever.

The Hon. ROBERT C. WINTHROP, who presided, then delivered the following introductory address: —

ADDRESS

BY THE HON. ROBERT C. WINTHROP.

WE are here, ladies and gentlemen, on this tenth day of November, in the year of our Lord 1883, under the auspices of the old Massachusetts Historical Society, to commemorate the four hundredth anniversary of the birthday of one of the greatest figures of modern history,—I might almost have said the very greatest.

Certainly, my friends, it may well be doubted whether, since the birth of that blessed Saviour, from whose nativity the years of our Christian calendar take their date, — as if there were no time worthy of being calculated or counted until Christ brought life and immortality to light, — it may well be doubted, I say, whether, since the incarnation of our Lord and the miraculous ministry of his great apostles, any one man has exerted so pervading and so powerful an influence on the condition and welfare of the human race as that son of a humble miner, who drew his first breath in the little German village of Eisleben four hundred years ago to-day.

The late eminent philosopher and diplomatist, Baron von Bunsen, spoke for all Germany in pronouncing Luther emphatically and unqualifiedly "the greatest hero of Christendom since the apostles." England might have been heard, two centuries and a half earlier, through the voice of John Milton, — no mean judge of human greatness, — speaking of him as one "whom God made choice of, before others, to be of highest eminence and power in reforming the Church." And, within a few months past, the historian Froude has said : " Had there been no Luther, the English, American, and German peoples would be thinking differently, would be acting differently, and would be altogether different men and women from what they are at this moment."

We do not forget, and Froude did not forget, that when Luther was born our Western Hemisphere was an unknown and undiscovered region of the earth. There was no America, North, South, or Central, on the map of the world at that day. Columbus and Vespucius, indeed, were already mature men, and Sebastian Cabot was six or seven years old. But nine years were still to elapse before Columbus landed at San Salvador or Samana, and five more years before John Cabot and his son Sebastian discovered the North American continent; while two more years still remained before Americus Vespucius reached South America, and afforded the pretext for giving his name to the whole New World.

That whole New World for another full century was without civilized Christian occupation. Not, indeed, till sixty-one years after Luther's death was the earliest English settlement at Jamestown; not till seventy-four years after his death was the landing of the Pilgrims at Plymouth; not till eighty-four years after his death was the founding of Boston and Massachusetts. Even St. Augustine, the first permanent Christian settlement in what is now our Country, dates from 1565, while Luther died in 1546. And yet, as I need not say, in the face of all these facts and figures, we are here to-day to recognize Martin Luther as, beyond all other men, the instrument of God in giving the impulse, by thought, word, and act, to that world-wide movement which resulted not merely in the reformation of Europe, but in all that we Americans now enjoy, and all that we rejoice in being. Pilgrim and Puritan, Cavalier and Roundhead, Huguenot and Quaker, yes, and Roman Catholic also, consciously or unconsciously, all alike felt that impulse, and American colonization and the American Revolution were among its results.

The venerable Emperor William, at the recent unveiling of the great Germania statue, opened a speech, as remarkable for condensed and comprehensive brevity and felicity as that of Abraham Lincoln at Gettysburg, with these words: "When Providence desires to signify its will with regard to mighty events upon the earth, it selects the time, countries, and instruments to accomplish its purpose." Those words belonged pre-eminently to the great Luther monument at Worms, the grandest monument in Europe, and which appeals to the admiration and sympathy of all who behold it, of whatever nation or tongue.

No local or limited celebrity, certainly, is sufficient for Luther, or commensurate with his fame. Not as a wonderful German, though he was the most wonderful of all Germans; not as the antagonist of Leo X. or of Charles V.; not as nailing theses to a church door, or burning a Papal bull at Wittenberg; not as braving an imperial diet at Worms; not even, only, as translating the Holy Scriptures at the Wartburg, and opening the Bible to all who had eyes to read it, — though that is glory enough for any man; — not for all or any of these characteristic incidents in his career, do we come to commemorate his birthday.   Still less do we come to indorse all his peculiarities of doctrine or all his violences of diction.   No sectarian, or even merely Protestant, views enter into this commemoration.

But we come as students of history, and in just recognition of historical truth, to hail the advent, and do grateful homage to the memory, and listen to the inspiring story, of a mighty instrument of God in awakening and rousing and reforming the world for all time and for all places beneath the sun; a man of indomitable courage and of unwavering faith in Christ, who kindled a flame of spiritual liberty never to be extinguished, but which is to burn brighter and brighter until the perfect day.

But it is not for me, my friends, to dwell on these topics. I am here only, as president of this Society, to present to you the chosen orator of the occasion; and I can do so in no more just or felicitous terms than those of my friend, Dr. George E. Ellis, who, in originally proposing this commemoration, said as follows: "Happily we have one with us who was for many years our associate in this Society, and a professor in the University, a German scholar, profoundly versed in the literature, the philosophy, the history, science, art, and broadest culture of the birth-land of Luther; and who is gifted with especial talents, with breadth of thought and compass of view, for a brilliant rehearsal of his career, and of his place in the world's history and in the higher development of humanity."

I have now the privilege of calling on the Rev. Dr. FREDERIC HENRY HEDGE.

Dr. HEDGE then rose, and spoke for nearly an hour and a half, without manuscript or notes, as follows: —

COMMEMORATIVE DISCOURSE

BY DR. FREDERIC H. HEDGE.

THE power which presides over human destiny and shapes the processes of history is wont to conceal its ulterior purpose from the agents it employs, who, while pursuing their special aims and fulfilling their appointed tasks, are, unknown to themselves, initiating a new era, founding a new world.

Such significance attaches to the name of Luther, one of that select band of providential men who stand conspicuous among their contemporaries as makers of history. For the Protestant Reformation which he inaugurated is very imperfectly apprehended if construed solely as a schism in the Church, a new departure in religion. In a larger view, it was our modern world, with its social developments, its liberties, its science, its new conditions of being, evolving itself from the old.

It would be claiming too much to assume that all of good which distinguishes these latter centuries from mediæval time is wholly due to that one event; that humanity would have made no progress in science and the arts of life but for Luther and his work. Other, contemporary agencies, independent of the rupture with Rome, — the printing-press, the revival of letters, the discovery of a new continent, and other geographical and astronomical findings, — have had their share in the regeneration of secular life.

But this we may safely assert: that the dearest goods of our estate — civil independence, spiritual emancipation, individual scope, the large room, the unbound thought, the free pen, whatever is most characteristic of this New England of our inheritance — we owe to the Saxon reformer in whose name we are here to-day.

A compatriot of Luther, the critic-poet Lessing, has made us familiar with the idea of an Education of the Human Race. Vico had previously affirmed a law of historic development, and inferred from that law a progressive improvement of man's estate. Lessing supplemented the New Science of Vico with a more distinct recognition of divine agency and an educating purpose in the method of history. But Lessing confined his view of divine education to the truths of religion. For these the school is the Church. But religion is only one side of human nature. Man as a denizen of this earthly world has secular interests and a secular calling which may, in some future synthesis, be found to be the necessary complement of the spiritual, — the other pole of the same social whole, — but meanwhile require for their right development and full satisfaction another school, co-ordinate with but independent of the Church. That school is the nation.

Now the nation, in the ages following the decline of Rome, had had no proper status in Christian history. There were peoples — Italian, French, English, German — distributed in territorial groups, but no nation, no polity conterminous with the territorial limits of each country, compacted and confined by those limits, having its own independent sovereign head. France, Germany, England, were mere geographical expressions. The peoples inhabiting these countries had a common head in the Bishop of Rome, whose power might be checked by the rival German Empire when the emperor was a man of force, a veritable ruler of men, and the papal incumbent an imbecile, but who, on the whole, was acknowledged supreme. Europe was ecclesiastically one ; and the ecclesiastical over-ruled, absorbed, the civil.

But already, before the birth of Luther, from the dawn of the fourteenth century, the civil power had begun to disengage itself from the spiritual. The peoples here and there had consolidated into nations. Philip of France had defied the Pope of his day, and hurled him from his throne. The Golden Bull had made the German Empire independent of papal dictation in the choice of its incumbents. Meanwhile the Babylonish Captivity and subsequent dyarchy in the pontificate had sapped the prestige of the Roman see. As we enter the fifteenth century, we find the principle of nationality formally recognized by the Church. At the Council of Constance, the assembly decided to vote by nations instead of dioceses, each nation having a distinct voice. Then it appeared that the nation had become a reality and a power in Christendom.

Another century was needed to break the chain which bound in ecclesiastical dependence on Rome the nations especially charged with the conduct of mankind. And a man was needed who had known from personal experience the stress of that chain, and whose moral convictions were too exigent to allow of compliance and complicity with manifest falsehood and deadly wrong. To ecclesiastical severance succeeded political. To Martin Luther, above all men, we Anglo-Americans are indebted for national independence and mental freedom.

It is from this point of view, and not as a teacher of religious truth, that he claims our interest. As a theologian, as a thinker, he has taught us little. Men of inferior note have contributed vastly more to theological enlightenment and the science of religion. Intellectually narrow, theologically bound and seeking to bind, his work was larger than his vision and better than his aim. The value of his thought is inconsiderable; the value of his deed as a providential liberator of thought is beyond computation.

The world has no prevision of its heroes. Nature gives no warning when a great man is born. Had any soothsayer undertaken to point out, among the children cast upon the world in electoral Saxony on the 10th of November, 1483, the one who would shake Christendom to its centre, this peasant babe, just arrived in the cottage of Hans Luther at Eisleben, might have been the last on whom his prophecy would have fallen. The great man is unpredictable; but reflection finds in the birth of Luther a peculiar fitness of place and time. Fitness of place, inasmuch as Frederick the Wise, Elector of Saxony, his native prince and patron, was probably the only one among the potentates of that day who, from sympathy and

force of character, possessed the will and the ability to shield
the reformer from prelatical wiles and the wrath of Rome;
Fitness of time, — a generation had scarcely gone by since the
newly invented printing-press had issued its first Bible; and
during the very year of this nativity, in 1483, Christopher
Columbus was making his first appeals for royal aid in real-
izing his dream of a western hemisphere hidden from European
ken behind the waves of the Atlantic, where the Protestant
principle, born of Luther, was destined to find its most con-
genial soil and to yield its consummate fruit.

More important than fitness of time and place is the adap-
tation of the man to his appointed work.   There is an easy,
levelling theory, held by some, that men are the product of
their time, great actors the necessary product of extraordinary
circumstances; that Cæsar and Mohammed and Napoleon,
had they not lived precisely when they did, would have plod-
ded through life and slipped into their graves without a
record; and that, on the other hand, quite ordinary men, if
thrown upon the times in which those heroes lived, would
have done as they did and accomplished the same results, —
would have overthrown the Roman aristocracy, abolished
idolatry, and brought order out of chaotic revolution.

But man and history are not, I think, to be construed so.
There is a law which adapts the man to his time.   The work
to be done is not laid upon a chance individual; the availing
of the crisis is not left to one who happens to be on the spot;
but from the foundation of the world the man was selected to
stand just there, and to do just that.   The opportunity does
not make the man, but finds him.   He is the providential
man; all the past is in him, all the future is to flow from him.

What native qualifications did Luther bring to his work?
First of all, his sturdy Saxon nature.   The Saxons are Germans of the Germans, and Luther was a Saxon of the Saxons;
reverend, patient, laborious, with quite an exceptional power
of work and capacity of endurance; simple, humble; no
visionary, no dreamer of dreams, but cautious, conservative,
incorruptibly honest, true to the heart's core; above all, cour-
ageous, firm, easily led when conscience seconded the leading,

impossible to drive when conscience opposed, ecstatically devout, tender, loving, — a strange compound of feminine softness and adamantine inflexibility. Contemporary observers noticed in the eyes of the man, dark, flashing, an expression which they termed demonic. It is the expression of one susceptible of supernatural impulsion, — of being seized and borne on by a power which exceeds his conscious volition.

In this connection I have to speak of one property in Luther which especially distinguishes spiritual heroes, — the gift of faith. The ages which preceded his coming have been called "the ages of faith." The term is a misnomer if understood in any other sense than that of blind acquiescence in external authority, unquestioning submission to the dictum of the Church. This is not faith, but the want of it, mental inaction, absence of independent vision. Faith is essentially active, a positive, aggressive force ; not a granter of current propositions, but a maker of propositions, of dispensations, of new ages.

Faith is not a constitutional endowment; there is no lot or tumulus assigned to it among the hillocks of the brain. It is not a talent connate with him who has it, and growing with his growth, but a gift of the Spirit, communicated to such as are charged with a providential mission to their fellow-men. It is the seal of their indenture, the test of their calling. In other words, faith is inspiration ; it is the subjective side of that incalculable force of which inspiration is the objective. So much faith, so much inspiration, so much of Deity.

Inspiration is in no man a constant quantity. In Luther it appears unequal, intermittent ; ebb and flood, but always, in the supreme crises of his history, answering to his need ; a master force, an ecstasy of vision and of daring ; lifting him clean out of himself, or rather eliciting, bringing to the surface, and forcing into action the deeper, latent self of the man, against all the monitions not only of prudence, but of conscience as well. The voice of worldly prudence is soon silenced by earnest souls intent on noble enterprises of uncertain issue. What reformer of traditional wrongs has not been met by the warning, "That way danger lies"? But in Luther we

have the rarer phenomenon of conscience itself overcome by faith. We have the amazing spectacle of a righteous man defying his own conscience in obedience to a higher duty than conscience knew. For conscience is the pupil of custom, the slave of tradition, bound by prescription ; the safeguard of the weak, but, it may be, an offence to the strong ; wanting initiative ; unable of itself to lift itself to new perceptions and new requirements, whereby " enterprises of great pith and moment" "their currents turn awry, and lose the name of action." Conscience has to be new-born when a new dispensation is given to the world. It was only thus that Christianity through Paul could disengage itself from Judaism, which had the old conscience on its side.

In Luther faith was stronger than conscience. Had it not been so, we should not be here to-day to celebrate his name. Of all his trials in those years of conflict, which issued in final separation from Rome, the struggle with conscience was the sorest. However strong his personal conviction that indulgences bought with money could not save from the penalties of sin, that the sale of them was a grievous wrong, to declare that conviction, to act upon it, was to pit himself against the head of the Church, to whom he owed unconditional allegiance. It was revolt against legitimate authority, a violation of his priestly vows. So conscience pleaded. But Luther's better moments set aside these scruples, regarding them, as he did all that contradicted his strong intent, as suggestions of the Devil. "How," whispered Satan, "if your doctrine be erroneous, — if all this confusion has been stirred up without just cause? How dare you preach what no one has ventured for so many centuries? "

Over all these intrusive voices admonishing, " You must not," a voice more imperative called to him, " You must ; " and a valor above all martial daring responded, " I will." Here is where a higher power comes in to reinforce the human. When valor in a righteous cause rises to that pitch, it draws Heaven to its side; it engages Omnipotence to back it.

Our knowledge of Luther's history is derived in great part from his own reminiscences and confessions.

His boyhood was deeply shadowed by the sternness of domestic discipline. Severely and even cruelly chastised by conscientious but misjudging parents, more careful to inspire fear than to cherish filial love, he contracted a shyness and timidity which kept back for years the free development of a noble nature. At school it was still worse: the business of education was then conceived as a species of rhabdomancy, a divining by means of the rod the hidden treasures of the boyish mind. He cannot forget, in after years, that fifteen times in one day the rod, in his case, was so applied. " The teachers in those days," he says, " were tyrants and executioners ; the school, a prison and a hell."

At a more advanced school in Eisenach, where the sons of the poor supported themselves by singing before the doors of wealthy citizens, who responded with the fragments of their abundance, a noble lady, Dame Ursula Cotta, impressed by the fervor and vocal skill of the lad, gave him a daily seat at her table, and with it his first introduction to polite society, — a privilege which went far to compensate the adverse influences of his earlier years.

At the age of eighteen he entered the University of Erfurt, then the foremost seminary in Germany, the resort of students from all parts of the land. The improved finances of his father sufficed to defray the cost of board and books. He elected for himself the department of philosophy, then embracing, together with logic, metaphysic, and rhetoric, the study of the classics, which the recent revival of letters had brought into vogue. The Latin classics became his familiar friends, and are not unfrequently quoted in his writings. He made good·use of the golden years, and received in due order, with high distinction, the degrees of bachelor and of master of arts.

With all this rich culture and the new ideas with which it flooded his mind, it does not appear that any doubt had been awakened in him of the truth of the old religion. He was still a devout Catholic; he still prayed to the saints as the proper helpers in time of need. When accidentally wounded by the sword which according to student fashion he wore at his side, lying, as he thought, at the point of death, he invoked not God, but the Virgin, for aid. "Mary, help!" was his cry.

He was destined by his father for the legal profession. It was the readiest road to wealth and power. Accordingly, he applied himself with all diligence to the study of law, and had fitted himself for the exercise of that calling, when suddenly, in a company of friends assembled for social entertainment, he announced his intention to quit the world and embrace the monastic life. They expressed their astonishment at this decision, and endeavored to dissuade him from such a course. In vain they urged him to reconsider his purpose. "Farewell!" he said. "We part to meet no more."

What was it that caused this change in Luther's plan of life? To account for a turn apparently so abrupt, it must be remembered that his religion hitherto, the fruit of his early training, had been a religion of fear. He had been taught to believe in an angry God, and the innate, deep corruption of human nature. He was conscious of no crime; no youthful indiscretions, even, could he charge himself with; but morbid self-scrutiny presented him utterly sinful and corrupt. Only a life of good works could atone for that corruption. Such a life the monastic, with its renunciations, its prayers and fastings and self-torture, was then believed to be, — a life well pleasing in the sight of God, the surest way of escape from final perdition. Exceptional virtue tended in that direction. To be a monk was to flee from wrath and attain to holiness and heaven.

All this had lain dimly, half consciously, in Luther's mind, not ripened into purpose. The purpose was precipitated by a searching experience. Walking one day in the neighborhood of Erfurt, he was overtaken by a terrific thunderstorm. The lightning struck the ground at his feet. Falling on his knees, he invoked, in his terror, the intercession of St. Anna, and vowed, if life were spared, to become a monk. Restored to his senses, he regretted the rash vow. His riper reason in after years convinced him that a vow ejaculated in a moment of terror imposed no moral obligation;

but his uninstructed conscience could not then but regard it' as binding. In spite of the just and angry remonstrances of his father, who saw with dismay his cherished plan defeated, the hard-earned money spent on his boy's education expended in vain, he sought and gained admission to the brotherhood and cloisters of St. Augustine at Erfurt.

His novitiate was burdened with cruel trials. The hardest and most repulsive offices were laid upon the new-comer, whose superiors delighted to mortify the master of arts with disgusting tasks. To the stern routine of cloister discipline he added self-imposed severities, more frequent fastings and watchings, undermining his health, endangering life. Harder to bear than all these were his inward conflicts, — fears and fightings, agonizing self-accusations, doubts of salvation, apprehensions of irrevocable doom. He sought to conquer heaven by mortification of the flesh, and despaired of the result. Finally, encouraged by Staupitz, the vicar-general of the order, and guided by his own study of the new-found Scriptures, he came to perceive that heaven is not to be won in that way. Following the lead of St. Paul and Augustine, he reached the conclusion which formed thenceforth the staple of his theology and the point of departure in his controversy with Rome, — the sufficiency of divine grace, and justification by his faith.

In the second year of his monastic life he was ordained priest, and in the year following promoted to the chair of theology in the new University of Wittenberg, where he soon became famous as a preacher.

In 1511 he was sent on a mission to Rome, in company with a brother monk. When he came within sight of the city he fell upon his knees and saluted it: "Hail, holy Rome, thrice consecrated by the blood of the martyrs!" Arrived within the walls, the honest German was inexpressibly shocked by what he found in the capital of Christendom, — open infidelity, audacious falsehood, mockery of sacred things, rampant licentiousness, abominations incredible. The Rome of Julius II. was the *Roma rediviva* of Caligula and Nero, — pagan in spirit, pagan in morals, a sink of iniquity. It was

4

well that Luther had personal experience of all this; the remembrance of it served to lighten the struggle with conscience, when called to contend against papal authority. But then such contest never entered his mind; he was still a loyal son of the Church. He might mourn her corruption, but would not question her infallibility. Like other pilgrims zealous of good works, he climbed on his knees the twenty-eight steps of the Santa Scala. While engaged in that penance there flashed on his mind, like a revelation from heaven, declaring the futility of such observances, the saying of the prophet, "The just shall live by his faith."

Returned to Wittenberg, he was urged by Staupitz to study for the last and highest academic honor, that of doctor of philosophy. The already overtasked preacher shrank from this new labor. "Herr Staupitz," he said, "it will be the death of me." "All right," answered Staupitz. "Our Lord carries on extensive operations; he has need of clever men above. If you die you will be one of his councillors in heaven."

I now come to the turning-point in Luther's life, — the controversy with Rome on the subject of indulgences, which ended in the schism known as the Protestant Reformation.

Leo X., in the year 1516, ostensibly in the interest of a new church of St. Peter in Rome, sent forth a bull according absolution from the penalties of sin to all who should purchase the indulgences offered for sale by his commissioners. Indulgence, according to the theory of the Church, was dispensation from the penance otherwise required for priestly absolution. It was not pretended that priestly absolution secured divine forgiveness and eternal salvation. It was absolution from temporal penalties due to the Church; but popular superstition identified the one with the other. Moreover, it was held that the supererogatory merits of Christ and the saints were available for the use of sinners. They constituted a treasury confided to the Church, whose saving virtue the head of the church could dispense at discretion. In this case the application of that fund was measured by pecuniary equivalents. Christ had said, "How hardly shall they that have riches enter the kingdom of heaven." Leo said in effect, " How easily may they that have riches enter the kingdom of heaven," since they have the *quid pro quo*. For the poor it was not so easy ; and this was one aspect of the case which stimulated the opposition of Luther. Penitence was nominally required of the sinner, but proofs of penitence were not exacted. Practically, the indulgence meant impunity for sin. A more complete travesty of the gospel — laughable, if not so impious — could hardly be conceived. The faithful themselves were shocked by the shameless realism which characterized the proclamations of the German commissioner, Tetzel.

Luther wrote a respectful letter to the Archbishop of Mainz, praying him to put a stop to the scandal; little dreaming that the prelate had a pecuniary interest in the business, having bargained for half the profits of the sale as the price of his sanction of the same. Other dignitaries to whom he appealed refused to interfere. As a last resource, by way of appeal to the Christian conscience, on the 31st of October, 1517, he nailed his famous ninety-five theses to the door of the church of All Saints. These were not dogmatic assertions, but propositions to be debated by any so inclined. Nevertheless, the practical interpretation put upon them was the author's repudiation of indulgences, and, by implication, his arraignment of the source from which they emanated.

It is doubtful if Luther apprehended the full significance of the step he had taken. He did not then dream of secession from the Church. He was more astonished than gratified when he learned that his theses and other utterances of like import had, within the space of fourteen days, pervaded Germany, and that he had become the eye-mark of Christendom. More than once before the final irrevocable act he seems to have regretted his initiative, and though he would not retract he would fain have sunk out of sight.

But fortunately for the cause, Tetzel, baffled in his designs on Luther's congregation, attacked him with such abusive virulence and extravagant assertions of papal authority that

Luther was provoked to rejoin with more decisive declarations. The controversy reached the ear of the Pope, who inclined at first to regard it as a local quarrel, which would soon subside, but was finally persuaded to despatch a summons requiring Luther to appear in Rome within sixty days, to be tried for heresy. Rome might summon, but Luther knew too well the probable result of such a trial to think of obeying the summons. The spiritual power might issue its mandates, but the temporal power was needed to execute its behests. Would the temporal, in this case, co-operate with the spiritual? There had been a time when no German potentate would have hesitated to surrender a heretic. But Germany was getting tired of Roman dictation and ultramontane insolence. The German princes were getting impatient of the constant drain on their exchequer by a foreign power. Irrespective of the right or wrong of his position, theologically considered, the question of Luther's extradition was one of submission to authority long felt to be oppressive. Only personal enemies, like Eck and Emser and Tetzel, would have him sent to Rome. Miltitz, who had been deputed to deal with him, confessed that an army of twenty-five thousand men would not be sufficient to take him across the Alps, so widespread and so powerfully embodied was the feeling in his favor. The Ritter class, comprising men like Franz von Sickingen and Ulrich von Hutten, were on his side; so were the humanists, apostles of the new culture, which opposed itself to the old mediæval scholasticism. The Emperor Maximilian would have the case tried on German soil. Conspicuous above all, his chief defender, was Luther's own sovereign, the Elector of Saxony, Frederick the Wise. Humanly speaking, but for him the Reformation would have been crushed at the start, and its author with it. Frederick was not at this time a convert to Luther's doctrine, but insisted that his subject should not be condemned until tried by competent judges and refuted on scriptural grounds. He occupied the foremost place among the princes of Germany. On the death of Maximilian, 1519, he was regent of the empire, and had the chief voice in the election of the new emperor. Without his consent and co-operation it was impossible for Luther's enemies to get possession of his person. For this purpose, Leo X., then Pope, wrote a flattering letter, accompanied by the coveted gift of the "golden rose," supreme token of pontifical good-will. "This rose," wrote Leo, "steeped in a holy chrism, sprinkled with sweet-smelling musk, consecrated by apostolic blessing, symbol of a sublime mystery, — may its heavenly odor penetrate the heart of our beloved son, and dispose him to comply with our request."

The request was not complied with, but by way of alternative it was proposed that Luther should be tried by a papal commissioner in Germany. So Leo despatched for that purpose the Cardinal de Vio, of Gaeta, his plenipotentiary, commonly known as Cajetan. A conference was held at Augsburg, which, owing to the legate's passionate insistence on unconditional retractation, served but to widen the breach. The efforts of Miltitz, another appointed mediator, met with no better success.

Meanwhile Luther had advanced with rapid and enormous strides in the line of divergence from the Catholic Church. The study of the Scriptures had convinced him that the primacy of the Roman bishop had no legitimate foundation. The work of Laurentius Valla, exposing the fiction of Constantine's pretended donation of temporal sovereignty in Rome, had opened his eyes to other falsehoods. He proclaimed his conclusions, writing and publishing in Latin and German with incredible diligence. His Address to the Christian Nobility of the German Nation, concerning the Melioration of the Christian State, the most important of his publications, anticipates nearly all the points of the Protestant reform, and many which were not accomplished in Luther's day. The writing spread and sped through every province of Germany, as if borne on the wings of the wind. An edition of four thousand copies was exhausted in a few days. It was the Magna Charta of a new ecclesiastical state.

But now the thunderbolt was launched which, his adversaries trusted, should smite the heretic to death and scatter

all his following. On the 16th of June, 1520, Leo issued a
bull condemning Luther's writings, commanding that they
be publicly burned wherever found, and that their author,
unless within the space of sixty days he recanted his errors,
allowing sixty more for the tidings of his recantation to reach
Rome, should be seized and delivered up for the punishment
due to a refractory heretic. All magistrates and all citizens
were required, on pain of ecclesiastical penalty, to aid in
arresting him and his followers and sending them to Rome.
The papal legates, Aleander and Caraccioli, were appointed
bearers of a missive from the Pope to Duke Frederick, commanding him to have the writings of Luther burned, and
either to execute judgment on the heretic himself, or else to
deliver him up to the papal tribunal. The Elector replied
that he had no part in Luther's movement, but that his writings must be refuted before he would order their burning;
that their author had been condemned unheard; that his
case must be tried by impartial judges in some place where it
should be safe for him to appear in person.

Miltitz persuaded Luther, as a last resource, to write to
the Pope a conciliatory letter, disavowing all personal hos-
tility and expressing due reverence for his Holiness. He
did write. But such a letter! An audacious satire, which,
under cover of personal respect and good-will, compassion-
ates the Pope as "a sheep among wolves," and characterizes
the papal court as "viler than Sodom or Gomorrah."

When the bull reached Wittenberg it was treated by
Luther and his friends with all the respect which it seemed
to them to deserve. On the 10th of December, 1520, a large
concourse of students and citizens assembled in the open
space before the Elster gate; a pile was erected and fired by
a resident graduate of the university, and on it Luther with
his own hands solemnly burned the. bull and the papal de-
cretals, amid applause which, like the "embattled farmers'"
shot at Concord in 1775, was "heard round the world."

So the last tie was severed which bound Luther to Rome.
After that contumacious act there was no retreat or possibil-
ity of pacification.

But though Luther had done with Rome, Rome had not yet done with him. When Leo found that he could not wrest the heretic from the guardianship of Frederick, he had recourse to imperial aid. The newly elected emperor, Charles V., a youth of twenty-one, in whose blood were blended three royal lines of devoted friends of the Church, might be expected to render prompt obedience to its head. But Charles was unwilling to break with Frederick, to whom he was chiefly indebted for his election. He would not, if he could, compel him to send Luther a prisoner to Rome. He chose to have him tried in his own court, and only when proved by such trial an irreclaimable heretic to surrender him as such.

An imperial Diet was about to be held at the city of Worms. Thither Charles desired the Elector to bring the refractory monk. Frederick declined the office; but Luther declared that if the emperor summoned him he would obey the summons as the call of God. To his friend Spalatin, who advised his refusal, he wrote that he would go to Worms if there were as many devils opposed to him as there were tiles on the roofs of the houses.

The summons came, accompanied by an imperial safe-conduct covering the journey to and from the place of trial. Luther complied; he had no fear that Charles would repeat the treachery of Sigismund, which had blasted that name with eternal infamy and incarnadined Bohemia with atoning blood. The journey was one triumphal progress; in every city ovations, not unmingled with cautions and regrets. He arrived in the morning of the 16th of April, 1521. The warder on the tower announced with the blast of a trumpet his approach. The citizens left their breakfasts to witness the entry. Preceded by the imperial herald and followed by a long cavalcade, the stranger was escorted to the quarters assigned him. Alighting from his carriage, he looked round upon the multitude and said, " God will be with me." It was then that Aleander, the papal legate, remarked the demonic glance of his eye. People of all classes visited him in his lodgings.

On the following day he was called to the episcopal palace, and made his first appearance before the Diet. A pile of books was placed before him. " Are these your writings? " The titles were called for, and Luther acknowledged them to be his. Would he retract the opinions expressed in them, or did he still maintain them? He begged time for consideration ; it was a question of faith, of the welfare of souls, of the word of God. A day for deliberation was allowed him, and he was remanded to his lodgings. On the way the people shouted applause, and a voice exclaimed, " Blessed is the womb that bare thee! " But the impression made on the court was not favorable. He had not shown the front that was expected of him. He had seemed timid, irresolute. The emperor remarked, " That man would never make a heretic of me."

His self-communings in the interim, and his prayer, which has come down to us, show how deeply he felt the import of the crisis; how " the fire burned," as he mused of its probable issue, knowing that the time was at hand when he might be called to seal his testimony with his blood.

" Ah, God, thou my God! stand by me against the reason and the wisdom of all the world! Thou must do it; it is not my cause, but thine. For my own person, I have nothing to do with these great lords of the earth. Gladly would I have quiet days and be unperplexed. But thine is the cause ; it is just and eternal. Stand by me, thou eternal God! I confide in no man. Hast thou not chosen me for this purpose, I ask thee?. But I know of a surety that thou hast chosen me."

On the 18th he was summoned for the second time, and the question of the previous day was renewed. He explained at length, first in Latin, then in German, that his writings were of various import : those which treated of moral topics the papists themselves would not condemn ; those which disputed papal authority and those addressed to private individuals, although the language might be more violent than was seemly, he could not in conscience revoke. Unless he were refuted from the Scriptures, he must abide by his opinions. He was told that the court was not there to discuss his opinions; they had been already condemned by the Council of Constance. Finally, the question narrowed itself to this: Did he believe that councils could err? More specifically, Did he believe the Council of Constance had erred? Luther appreciated the import of the question. He knew that his answer would alienate some who had thus far befriended him. For however they might doubt the infallibility of the Pope, they all believed councils to be infallible. But he did not hesitate. "I do so believe." The fatal word was spoken. The emperor said, "It is enough, the hearing is concluded."

The shades of evening had gathered over the assembly. To the friends of Luther they might seem to forebode the impending close of his earthly day. Then, suddenly, he uttered with a loud voice, in his native idiom, those words which Germany will remember while the city of Worms has one stone left upon another, or the river that laves her shall find its way to the German Ocean: "Hier steh' ich, ich kann nicht anders; Gott hilf mir! Amen!"

By the light of blazing torches the culprit was conducted from the council chamber, the Spanish courtiers hissing as he went, while among the Germans many a heart no doubt beat high in response to that brave ultimatum of their fellow-countryman.

With the consent of the emperor further negotiations were attempted in private, and Luther found it far more difficult to resist the kindly solicitations of friends and peacemakers than to brave the threats of his enemies. But he did resist; the trial was ended. The great ones of the earth had assailed a poor monk, now with menace, now with entreaty, and found him inflexible.

> "The tide of pomp
> That beats upon the high shore of this world"

had broken powerless against the stern resolve of a single breast.

The curtain falls; when next it rises we are in the Wartburg, the ancestral castle of the counts of Thüringen, where

St. Elizabeth, the fairest figure in the Roman calendar, dispensed the benefactions and bore the heavy burden of her tragic life. The emperor, true to his promise, had arranged for the safe return of Luther to Wittenberg, declaring, however, that, once returned, he would deal with him as a heretic. At the instigation, perhaps, of Frederick, the protecting escort was assailed on the way, and put to flight by an armed troop. Luther was taken captive, and borne in secret to the Wartburg, where, disguised as a knight, he might elude the pursuit of his enemies. While there he occupied himself with writing, and among other labors prepared his best and priceless gift to his country, his translation of the New Testament, afterward supplemented by his version of the Old.

A word here respecting the merits of Luther as a writer. His compatriots have claimed for him the inestimable service of founder of the German language. He gave by his writings to the New High German, then competing with other dialects, a currency which has made it ever since, with slight changes, the language of German literature, the language in which Kant reasoned and Goethe sang. His style is not elegant, but charged with a rugged force, a robust simplicity, which makes for itself a straight path to the soul of the reader. His words were said to be " half battles ;" call them rather whole victories, for they conquered Germany. The first condition of national unity is unity of speech. In this sense Luther did more for the unification of Germany than any of her sons, from Henry the Fowler to Bismarck. "We conceded," says Gervinus, " to no metropolis, to no learned society, the honor of fixing our language, but to the man who better than any other could hit the hearty, healthy tone of the people. No dictionary of an academy was to be the canon of our tongue, but that book by which modern humanity is schooled and formed, and which in Germany, through Luther, has become, as nowhere else, a people's book."

Returning to Wittenberg, when change of circumstance permitted him to do so with safety, he applied himself with boundless energy to the work of constructing a new, reformed church to replace the old ; preaching daily in one or another

city, writing and publishing incessantly, instituting public
schools, arranging a new service in German as substitute
for the Latin mass, compiling a catechism (a model in its
kind), a hymnal, and other appurtenances of worship. And,
like the Israelites on their return from Babylon, while build-
ing the new temple with one hand, he fought with the other,
contending against Münzer, Carlstadt, the mystics, the icono-
clasts, the anabaptists ; often, it must be confessed, with un-
reasonable, intolerant wrath, spurning all that would not
square with his theology, as when he rejected the fellowship
of the Swiss, who denied the Real Presence in the eucharist.
When the fury of the Peasants' War was desolating Germany,
he wielded a martial pen against both parties ; arraigning the
nobles for their cruel oppressions, reproving the peasants for
attempting to overcome evil with greater evil.

His reform embraced, along with other departures from
the old *régime*, the abolition of enforced celibacy of the priest-
hood. He believed the family life to be the true life for cleric
as well as lay. He advised the reformed clergy to take to
themselves wives, and in 1525, in the forty-third year of his
age, he encouraged the practice by his example. He married
Catherine von Bora, an escaped nun, for whom he had previously endeavored to find another husband. She was one of
the many who had been placed in convents against their will,
and forced to take the veil. It was no romantic attachment
which induced Luther to take this step, but partly the feeling
that the preacher's practice should square with his teaching,
and partly an earnest desire to gratify his father, whose will
he had so cruelly traversed in becoming a monk. To marry
was to violate his monastic vow; but he had long since convinced himself that a vow made in ignorance, under extreme
pressure, was not morally binding.

Pleasing pictures of Luther's domestic life are given us by
contemporary witnesses, and the reports of his table talk. In
the bosom of his family he found an asylum from the wearing
labors and never-ending conflicts of his riper years. There he
shows himself the tender father, the trusting and devoted
husband, the open-handed, gay, and entertaining host. His

Kätchen proved in every respect an all-sufficient helpmeet. And it needed her skilful economy and creative thrift to counterbalance his inconsiderate and boundless generosity. For never was one more indifferent to the things of this world, more sublimely careless of the morrow.

The remaining years of Luther's life were deeply involved in the fortunes of the Reformation, its struggles and its triumphs, its still advancing steps in spite of opposition from without and dissensions within. They developed no new features, while they added intensity to some of the old, notably to his old impatience of falsehood and contradiction. They exhibit him still toiling and teeming, praying, agonizing, stimulating, instructing, encouraging; often prostrate with bodily disease and intense suffering; and still, amid all disappointments, tribulations, and tortures, breasting and buffeting with high-hearted valor the adverse tide which often threatened to overwhelm him.

Thus laboring, loving, suffering, exulting, he reached his sixty-fourth year, and died on the 18th of February, 1546. The last words he uttered expressed unshaken confidence in his doctrine, triumphant faith in his cause.

By a fit coincidence death overtook him in Eisleben, the place of his birth, where he had been tarrying on a journey connected with affairs of the Church.

The Count Mansfeld, who with his noble wife had ministered to Luther in his last illness, desired that his mortal remains should be interred in his domain; but the Elector, now John Frederick, claimed them for the city of Wittenberg, and sent a deputation to take them in charge. In Halle, on the way, memorial services were held, in which the university and the magnates of the city took part. In all the towns through which the procession passed the bells were rung, and the inhabitants thronged to pay their respects to the great deceased. In Wittenberg a military cortege accompanied the procession to the church of the electoral palace, where the obsequies were celebrated with imposing demonstrations, and a mourning city sent forth its population to escort the body to the grave.

In the year following, the Emperor Charles, having taken the Elector prisoner, stood as victor beside that grave. The Duke of Alva urged that the bones of the heretic should be exhumed and publicly burned; but Charles refused. "Let him rest; he has found his judge. I war not with the dead."

I have presented our hero in his character of reformer. I could wish, if time permitted, to exhibit him in other aspects of biographical interest. I would like to speak of him as a poet, author of hymns, into which he threw the fervor and swing of his impetuous soul; as a musical composer, rendering in that capacity effective aid to the choral service of his church. I would like to speak of him as a humorist and satirist, exhibiting the playfulness and pungency of Erasmus without his cynicism; as a lover of nature, anticipating our own age in his admiring sympathy with the beauties of earth and sky; as the first naturalist of his day, a close observer of the habits of vegetable and animal life; as a leader in the way of tenderness for the brute creation. I would like also, in the spirit of impartial justice, to speak of his faults and infirmities, in which Lessing rejoiced, as showing him not too far removed from the level of our common humanity.

But these are points on which I am not permitted to dwell. That phase of his life which gives to the name of Luther its world-historic significance is comprised in the period extending from the year 1517 to the year 1529; from the posting of the ninety-five theses to the Diet of Spires, from whose decisions German princes, dissenting, received the name of Protestants, and which, followed by the league of Smalcald, assured the success of his cause.

And now, in brief, what was that cause? The Protestant Reformation, I have said, is not to be regarded as a mere theological or ecclesiastical movement, however Luther may have meant it as such. In a larger view, it was secular emancipation, deliverance of the nations that embraced it from an irresponsible theocracy, whose main interest was the consolidation and perpetuation of its own dominion.

A true theocracy must always be the ideal of society; that is, a social order in which God as revealed in the moral law shall be practically recognized, inspiring and shaping the polity of nations. All the Utopias from Plato down are schemes for the realization of that ideal. But the attempt to ground theocracy on sacerdotalism has always proved and must always prove a failure. The tendency of sacerdotalism is to separate sanctity from righteousness. It invests an order of men with a power irrespective of character; a power whose strength lies in the ignorance of those on whom it is exercised; a power which may be, and often, no doubt, is, exercised for good, but which, in the nature of man and of things, is liable to such abuses as that against which Luther contended, when priestly absolution was affirmed to be indispensable to salvation, and absolution was venal, when impunity for sin was offered for sale, when the alternative of heaven or hell was a question of money.

It is not my purpose to impugn the Church of Rome as at present administered, subject to the checks of modern enlightenment and the criticism of dissenting communions. But I cannot doubt that if Rome could recover the hegemony which Luther overthrew, could once regain the entire control of the nations, the same iniquities, the same abominations, which characterized the ancient rule would reappear. The theory of the Church of Rome is fatally adverse to the best interests of humanity, light, liberty, progress. That theory makes a human individual the rightful lord of the earth, all potentates and powers beside his rightful subjects.

Infallible the latest council has declared him. Infallible! The assertion is an insult to reason. Nay, more, it is blasphemy, when we think of the attribute of Deity vested in a Boniface VIII., an Alexander VI., a John XXIII. Infallible? No! forever no! Fallible, as human nature must always be.

Honor and everlasting thanks to the man who broke for us the spell of papal autocracy; who rescued a portion, at least, of the Christian world from the paralyzing grasp of a power more to be dreaded than any temporal despotism, — a power which rules by seducing the will, by capturing the conscience of its subjects, — the bondage of the soul! Luther alone, of all the men whom history names, by faith and courage, by all his endowments, — ay, and by all his limitations, — was fitted to accomplish that saving work, — a work whose full import he could not know, whose far-reaching consequences he had not divined. They shape our life. Modern civilization, liberty, science, social progress, attest the world-wide scope of the Protestant reform, whose principles are independent thought, freedom from ecclesiastical thrall, defiance of consecrated wrong. Of him it may be said, in a truer sense than the poet claims for the architects of mediæval minsters, " He builded better than he knew." Our age still obeys the law of that movement whose van he led, and the latest age will bear its impress. Here, amid the phantasms that crowd the stage of human history, was a grave reality, a piece of solid nature, a man whom it is impossible to imagine not to have been ; to strike whose name and function from the record of his time would be to despoil the centuries following of gains that enrich the annals of mankind.

Honor to the man whose timely revolt checked the progress of triumphant wrong ; who wrested the heritage of God from sacerdotal hands, defying the traditions of immemorial time ! He taught us little in the way of theological lore ; what we prize in him is not the teacher, but the doer, the man. His theology is outgrown, a thing of the past, but the spirit in which he wrought is immortal ; that spirit is evermore the renewer and saviour of the world.

The exercises were concluded by the Rev. HENRY M. DEXTER, D.D., who pronounced the benediction.

www.ingramcontent.com/pod-product-compliance
Lightning Source LLC
Chambersburg PA
CBHW021439090426
42739CB00009B/1550